TO CHANGE A PLANET

BY **Christina Soontornvat**

ILLUSTRATED BY **Rahele Jomepour Bell**

SCHOLASTIC PRESS * NEW YORK

Our

planet.

Big, tough,

dependable.

Our planet has spun through eons of time. Mere moments ago, we arrived.

One person.
Small, quiet,
insignificant.

But when one person,
and one person,

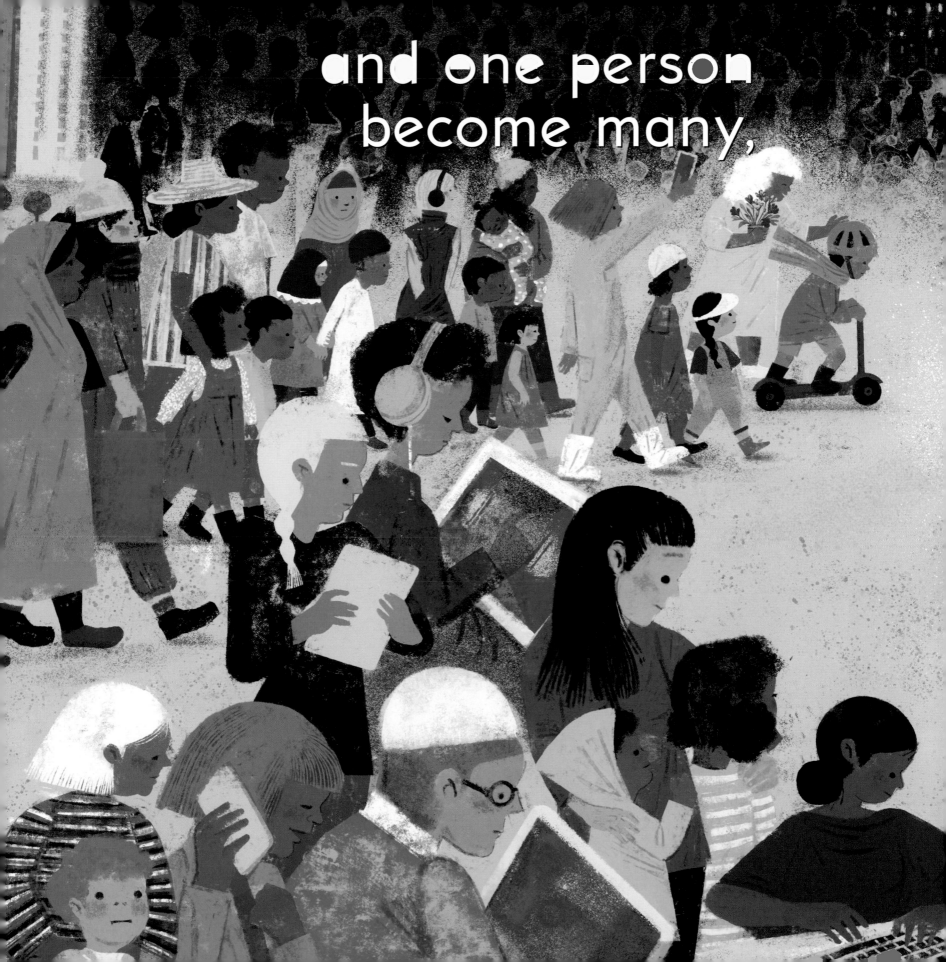

and one person
become many,

a planet.

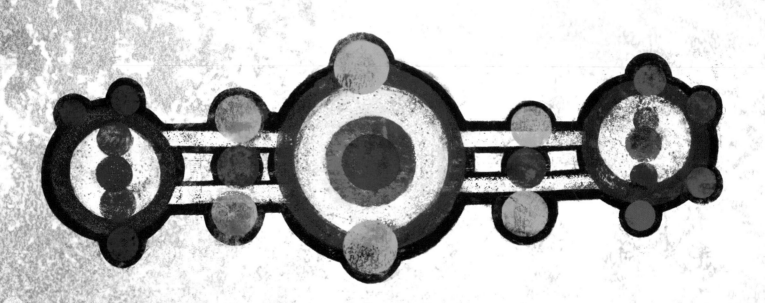

One molecule

of carbon

dioxide.

Small, quiet,

insignificant.

But when many cars,
many factories,
and many cities
let loose millions
and billions
and trillions,

they trap and stifle, like a too-warm blanket.

One notch higher on the thermometer. Small, quiet, insignificant.

But one notch higher
can change . . .

our
seas.

Our
seasons.

Life.

Us.

One person seems small,
quiet, and insignificant.
But when one person,

and one person, and one person

become many,

a planet.

Our planet seems tough, but it is fragile.

Our planet
seems big, but
it needs us.

Our planet has spun
through eons of time,
but this moment is the
one that matters most . . .

DEAR SENATOR,
I AM WRITING BECAUSE I CARE ABOUT THE CLIMATE CRISIS.
DAER GRANDMA,
I WENT TO MY VERY FIRST
CLIMATE MARCH YESTERDAY
This is me
DEAR CITY COUNCIL,
I SUPPORT THE NEW DOWNTOWN BIKE LANE PLAN.
TO MY REPRESENTATIVE,
PLEASE VOTE "YES" ON CLIMATE JUSTICE BILL.
DEAR NEIGHBOR,
HAVE YOU HEARD ABOUT OUR COMMUNITY COMPOST PROGRAM TO REDUCE FOOD WASTE?

for our planet,

our only home.

MORE ABOUT CLIMATE CHANGE

✳ WHAT IS CLIMATE CHANGE?

Weather refers to what is happening with the temperature, rain, and wind over the course of hours, days, or weeks. *Climate* tells you about the patterns in weather over longer periods of time. While weather can change by the hour, the climate on Earth has remained pretty steady for thousands of years.

But in just the last two centuries, humans have caused average temperatures on Earth to rise about 1° C (1.8° F) — enough to affect our planet's delicate ecosystems. Scientists warn that if the climate continues to warm too much and too quickly, it could have dire consequences for much of life on Earth.

✳ WHAT IS CAUSING CLIMATE CHANGE?

Throughout our planet's 4.5-billion-year history, our climate has changed because of natural factors, such as cycles of solar activity and volcanic eruptions. But the major cause of the current rise in global temperatures is human activity. Most factories, vehicles, and cities are powered by fossil fuels, including coal, petroleum, and natural gas. When these fossil fuels are used for energy, they release carbon gases, such as carbon dioxide and methane, into the atmosphere. These greenhouse gases are also released by deforestation and certain agricultural practices.

Greenhouse gases transmit sunlight to the earth's surface, and then trap some of the sun's heat in the atmosphere, warming our planet. Without the greenhouse effect, Earth would be too cold to sustain life as we know it. But an excess of greenhouse gases traps too much heat and leads to harmful levels of warming.

✳ HOW WILL RISING TEMPERATURES AFFECT LIFE ON EARTH?

Climate change is *already* affecting life on our planet. Our oceans have become warmer and more acidic. As the ice caps at the North and South poles melt, they are causing sea levels to rise. From fish to plankton, marine life is on the move, migrating to cooler waters and altering the fragile ecosystems of the ocean.

All over the globe, flowers and trees are budding earlier, and butterflies and birds are shifting their ranges because of rising temperatures. Animals that are unable to move, or have no safe habitat to move into, may be driven to extinction.

Humans are being affected, too. A warming planet causes weather to become more extreme. In general, dry places will continue to get drier, and wet places will become even wetter. Scientists predict that climate change will bring more heat waves, droughts, floods, and wildfires to places where humans live.

Mosquitoes and other pests are moving northward into areas that were once too cold for them, carrying diseases and parasites. Climate change will also affect our food supply, as crops, pests, and pollinators respond to rising temperatures. Global inequality puts the most vulnerable people—such as low-income communities and people of color—at the highest risk of suffering from a changing climate.

✳ HOW DO WE KNOW ALL THIS?

The most reliable source of scientific information about climate change comes from the United Nations' Intergovernmental Panel on Climate Change (IPCC). This group gathers evidence and information from thousands of researchers from all over the world.

Reports published by the IPCC are rigorously reviewed by experts, and include research from many different types of scientists, such as biologists, meteorologists, geologists, and specialists in disease prevention, economics, and agriculture. Some of the researchers have been gathering data for decades, which allows them to look at how our planet and our climate have changed over time. Other scientists develop computer models that simulate how climate change will affect our planet in the future. The overwhelming consensus of the IPCC is that *the planet is warming up, and human activities are the primary reason.*

✳ WHAT CAN WE DO TO TAKE ACTION?

One of the most important ways we can make an impact on climate change at home and in our communities is to create fewer greenhouse gases. Because many of us still get most of our energy from fossil fuels, this means lowering our energy use overall by driving less, eating more plants and less meat, conserving water, and making our homes more energy efficient. Producing new things requires energy, so we can buy less new stuff and reuse and recycle our old stuff.

These personal actions are very important, but climate change is such a big problem that it calls for big solutions. That may sound daunting, but humans have tackled some pretty serious problems in the past and succeeded by working together.

We can talk about climate change with our friends and neighbors and make sure they know where to find reliable sources of science-based information. We can hold companies accountable for their role in contributing to climate change. We can tell our leaders in local, state, and national governments that we expect them to take the health of our planet seriously by significantly cutting greenhouse gas emissions, investing in sustainable technologies such as wind and solar power, and rethinking the ways we use our land and feed ourselves. We must also prepare for life on a warming planet and make sure that marginalized communities don't bear the greatest burden of our already-changing climate.

Climate change is the biggest challenge we face today. But when one person, one person, and one person come together, we can do the work required to change our planet for the better.

✳ For my children, and for yours. —C. S.

✳ To all children, for whom and because of whom
planet Earth spins with love. —R. J. B.

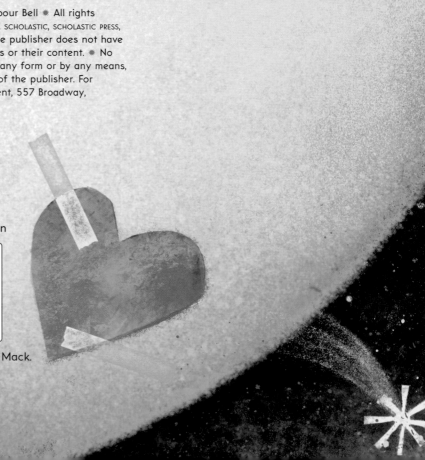

Thank you to Dr. Jay Banner of the University of Texas at Austin
for providing scientific expertise and guidance.

SOURCES

IPCC, 2014: *Climate Change 2014: Synthesis Report. Contribution of Working Groups I, II and III to
the Fifth Assessment Report of the Intergovernmental Panel on Climate Change* [Core Writing Team,
R. K. Pachauri and L. A. Meyer (eds.)]. IPCC, Geneva, Switzerland, 151 pp.

IPCC, 2018: Summary for Policymakers. In: *Global Warming of 1.5°C. An IPCC Special Report on the impacts
of global warming of 1.5°C above pre-industrial levels and related global greenhouse gas emission pathways,
in the context of strengthening the global response to the threat of climate change, sustainable development,
and efforts to eradicate poverty* [Masson-Delmotte, V., P. Zhai, H.-O. Pörtner, D. Roberts, J. Skea, P. R. Shukla, A. Pirani,
W. Moufouma-Okia, C. Péan, R. Pidcock, S. Connors, J. B. R. Matthews, Y. Chen, X. Zhou, M. I. Gomis, E. Lonnoy,
T. Maycock, M. Tignor, and T. Waterfield (eds.)]. World Meteorological Organization, Geneva, Switzerland, 32 pp.

Burke, K. D., Williams, J. W., Chandler, M. A., Haywood, A. M., Lunt, D. J., & Otto-Bliesner, B. L. (2018).
Pliocene and Eocene provide best analogs for near-future climates. *Proceedings of the National Academy of
Sciences of the United States of America, 115*(52), 13288–13293.

Parmesan, C., & Yohe, G. (2003). A globally coherent fingerprint of climate change impacts across natural systems.
Nature, 421, 37–42.

ISBN: 978-1-338-62861-6

10 9 8 7 6 5 4 3 2   22 23 24 25 26

Printed in China   38 ✳ First edition, August 2022

Rahele Jomepour Bell's art was created with gouache on paper, which was then
scanned and painted with digital brushes.
The text type and display type were set in SpaceRace Regular.
The book was printed on 128gsm SEN Matte art paper
50% REC FSC (50% virgin fiber + 50% post-consumer waste pulp),
and bound at RR Donnelley Asia.
Production was overseen by Jael Fogle.
Manufacturing was supervised by Shannon Rice.
The book was art directed and designed by Marijka Kostiw, and edited by Tracy Mack.

FSC
www.fsc.org
MIX
Paper from
responsible sources
FSC® C144853